Jac 5649/ ᔆ/11/o1

MW01141508

Dedication

My mother demonstrates **patience**

My dad demonstrates **assertiveness**

– the two essential qualities for *Thinking On Your Feet*

Acknowledgements

My special thanks go to my clients across the country whose work reinforces the increasing need for this skill and readers whose comments continue to refine the strategies.

HOW TO COMMUNICATE UNDER PRESSURE

Thinking On Your Feet

HOW TO COMMUNICATE UNDER PRESSURE
Thinking On Your Feet

Marian K. Woodall

JAICO PUBLISHING HOUSE
Mumbai ● Delhi ● Bangalore
Kolkata ● Hyderabad ● Chennai

© by Professional Business Communications

No part of this book may be reproduced or utilized in any form or by any means, electronic or mechanical including photocopying, recording or by any information storage and retrieval system, without permission in writing from the publishers.

Published in arrangement with:
Professional Business Communications
15800 SW Boones Ferry Road, Suite C-203,
Lake Oswego, Oregon 97035-3456,USA.

Org. Ttl. THINKING ON YOUR FEET
HOW TO COMMUNICATE UNDER PRESSURE
ISBN 81-7224-603-X

First Jaico Impression: 1997
Second Jaico Impression: 2001

Published by:
Jaico Publishing House
121, Mahatma Gandhi Road
Mumbai - 400 001.

Printed by:
Pramod Bhogate
Snehesh Printers
320-A, Shah & Nahar Ind. Est.–A-1,
Lower Parel, Mumbai - 400 013.

Contents

Preface

Thinking on your feet means considering what you want to communicate, so when you open your mouth, you are truly ready. Thinking on your feet means buying time before you speak. This book takes you though that entire process from thought to answer, from glimmer of idea to comment. It provides you with the keys to success: tools for buying time to do the thinking. It gives you interesting insights, a little theory and a great variety of examples to examine.

In the thirty years I've been talking to others about better communications, never has the need been greater for learning the skills and using the power that comes from saying what needs to be said, in a way the listener can hear it and understand it. These ideas began as a lecture called "Impromptu Responses." Webster defines *impromptu* as "without preparation; offhand." And that phrase clearly defines a problem in two communicating situations: when people are asked to speak unexpectedly and when they are asked a question. People who speak without thinking sufficiently sound unprepared. Sounding unprepared is a problem simply because you should be able to talk comfortably about whatever it is you are working on. Sounding unprepared lowers your poise, followed closely by a loss of confidence—both yours and your listener's. What happens next? You lose your credibility.

The premise of this book is that you could answer or comment well, if you thought briefly before you spoke.

These strategies for thinking before you speak have evolved through audience participation and reactions. Since the major concern of both clients and audiences continues to be how to answer questions, the primary focus is strategies and tips for responding better to questions, especially difficult ones. And to deal more successfully with questions it is important to know about questions, to observe the patterns of questions and what type of response each seeks (see chapter three). Understanding questions enables you to respond better–and you may even ask your own questions more carefully.

Critical to the discussion of questions and answers is an understanding of how successful communication occurs. The most frequent communication in business, as in personal and social lives, is conversation. For a conversation to be successful, more is needed than just questions and answers. Chapter three explains what else is needed.

A second focus is those unexpected opportunities to say a few words about something. My professional reaction is that no opportunity should be unexpected. When you are involved in a project, expect that someone will want to know how it's going, when it will be finished, what problems you've encountered, or how you feel about it. The point is that part of thinking on your feet occurs before you're asked.

New in this edition is a huge chapter on the job interview. In this era of multiple jobs, even multiple careers–it's more important than ever to be able to describe your experience in one career or area of your life to meet the requirements for a new career. It's also essential to understand how you make matchups that fit your background to the needs of the position. You also want to be able to sell yourself in the interview.

Finally, you'll find a chapter dealing with basic gender communications. It's important to understand that there **are**

differences in ways that men and women **tend** to communicate. With that background you can accomplish two worthwhile goals: 1) be more understanding of why people talk the way they do; 2) learn to modify your own favorite style to fit both the gender of the seeker and the situation of your conversation. This material is extracted from my book *How to Talk So Men Will Listen,* from a chapter called "The Conversational Wardrobe."

So, if your goal is communicating successfully with others, you will want to master thinking on your feet. If you are concerned about responding positively in tense situations—rather than saying something you later would give anything to take back—plan to master thinking on your feet. If you desire to appear poised and confident when put on the spot, learn how to think on your feet.

"Master" is the key word in your approach to the material. A quick reading will remind you of strategies to use when you need them, of ways to communicate that work. Readers call to say, *You know, Marian, I do lots of this stuff, but I didn't know why it worked.* Skimming the book will present specific new techniques for questions, responses, conversations. But if you wish to make the most of yourself, develop tools so that your approach becomes second nature. Then practice. Your results will be the three goals suggested in chapter one:

- Effective Communications
- Improved Human Relations
- Credibility and Poise.

Be poised and be powerful!

–Marian K. Woodall

1

What Is Thinking On Your Feet? and Why Is It Important?

Thinking on your feet is to say exactly what you want to say—whether you are standing or seated. To think on your feet is to say the appropriate thing at the right moment–during your conversation, not after you hang up the telephone or leave the room. Thinking on your feet means responding to all questions equally well. That promise includes three kinds of questions:

- Those you **can** answer, and want to
- Those you **could** answer, but prefer not to answer directly
- Those you **can't** answer.

Thinking on your feet means having credibility when you respond or speak extemporaneously. Thinking on your feet means sounding assertive when you wish not to be bested as a consumer. It means creating the best impression you can create when you interview for a job. To think on your feet is to remember both gender and situation when you make a comment. Thinking on your feet especially means responding to questions–all questions, both the routine and the challenging–equally well.

Thinking on your feet is **not** about "blowing smoke."

This important communication skills means being in control. It means appearing and sounding professional no matter who asks you a question, matter what the question is. It means appearing and sounding professional no matter where you are asked to make a comment and no matter what the comment is about.

Goals of Thinking On Your Feet

Plan three significant goals when you master thinking on your feet:

- Effective communications
- Improved human relationships
- Credibility and poise.

Communicating with others on a one-to-one basis is a fact of life and of work many people take for granted. We shouldn't. Effective communication means a great deal more than just getting the right words out. Certainly part of communication is the words. But more of it is the non verbal message which surrounds the words.

Nonverbal communication is so important, in fact, that if you are receiving a mixed message–the words communicate one message, the nonverbal another–the nonverbal message will usually be the truer one. How does all this relate to thinking on your feet? It's basic: if you blurt out the first thing that comes to your mind, without thought or planning, you are often faced with results you do not like. And if you say something that is not true, your non verbal message will contradict your words.

So, thinking on your feet also means being confident that all of what you communicate is appropriate: your verbal message will be consistent with your nonverbal message. Your communication will be effective, your human relations will be good, and your poise and credibility will be intact, even enhanced.

An Easy Skill To Master

Saying the appropriate thing at the appropriate time is a skill most everyone can master. Learn to think on your feet with the same unconscious ease with which you hit a great golf shot, bake a perfect pie crust, close a difficult sale, or interpret a balance sheet. With practice you can think on your feet without having to "think" about what tools are involved.

Learning This Communication Skill

As in learning any skill, there are two basic steps: learn the techniques and practice them. In this book you will learn tips for general success and the specific techniques or tactics to use when in various difficult communications situations. Plan to practice these techniques by yourself, with your family, your colleagues, your friends, until the techniques become second nature. Use an audio tape or video tape to hear and see what areas you have mastered and areas where you need to improve. Another easy opportunity for practice occurs when you leave a voice mail message. After you leave your message, most systems include this message: "Press one for more options." One of the options is to listen to the message you just left. Not only can you quickly hear how you sound, you can rerecord it. Take advantage of this quick, easy chance to check yourself and to improve. Then practice, practice, practice.

Why Is it Important To Think On Your Feet?

Thinking on your feet is important for reasons you already know: confidence, credibility, appearing and sounding professional, making an impressive appearance, looking and sounding unflappable, being known as a person to rely on in a difficult situation.

What about confidence? You have to be confident to think on your feet successfully. How can that also increase confidence? The fact that you know you can do it makes you more confident in all other communications activities. Knowing you won't be embarrassed adds to that confident feeling. Realizing others won't be able to put you down or leave you at a loss for words further enhances your confident feeling.

What about credibility? To have credibility, your words and the surrounding nonverbal messages need to fit. That means your voice, your posture, your timing, and your demeanor reinforce your words, not contradict them.

Appearing and sounding professional? No one knows all the answers all the time. But don't your customers (or your students, your subordinates, your clients) think you should? How do you look (and feel) when you are asked a question which you must hedge in responding to? When hedging, it's even more important to remain in control, to maintain people's trust and respect—and their business. When people ask questions, what they often want to know is *Are you reliable? Are you in charge here? Do you know what you're talking about? Will my money (or stocks, or automobile, or clothes, or kids) be safe with you?*

Creating an impression? The impression you leave with people is frequently much more important than the information you give them. Nonverbal gestures, delivery (including speed, emphasis, and tone), body posture all send the impression the customer or client receives and responds to. Thinking on your feet enables you to be certain the impression they receive is positive. People think, *She's very professional. He knows what he's doing.*

Appearing unflappable? When you are a person others can't fluster, they'll soon learn that and quit trying. If being asked direct, pointed questions no longer puts you on the spot, people will tend not to ask them. If being called upon unexpectedly does not throw you, you'll be considered unflappable. An unflappable person is relied upon and admired. Reactions tend to be *Say, you can't catch him napping. He's on top of everything.* or *I admire a person who handles things without getting all bent out of shape.*

How about being known as a person who can be relied upon in a difficult situation? You are the people who are given more responsibility, quicker promotions, awarded difficult or risky client contacts which pay such fine dividends when they are successfully handled. Your boss's reaction, *Jane's the person for the Folger Brothers; with her abilities to answer their picky little questions, she'll get that account for sure.*

Learning how to think on your feet will reward you in more ways than you can imagine. Resolve today to learn the tools and develop this skill of *Thinking On Your Feet.*

2

Do You Need To Think On Your Feet?

Yes.

Does your job require you to answer questions frequently? Thinking on your feet quickly and appropriately is the secret to success in that portion of your job. Answering well the first time solves problems, forestalls follow-up questions, and enables you to be more productive. You need to think on your feet if you provide a professional service to others as a doctor, lawyer, consultant, accountant.

If you speak to the press—that means politician, bureau chief, community relations coordinator, media liaison, public relations specialist, marketing executive, City Council member, candidate for office—you need to think before you speak. If you are answerable to a Board of Directors or to stockholders, thinking on your feet is a requirement in your job description. Won't you be proud when you can smile warmly at that old timer who tries to pin you down at the annual meeting? You can dispatch his whiny, negative question with a firm, positive response.

You also need to speak well on your feet if you are a sales representative who calls on clients, a retail sales clerk who deals with customers, or a counter person in any service industry or organization which deals with the public. Consider this positive response to a customer complaint:

> *Yes, Mr. Jones, I can certainly understand that it seemed to be taking the service technician a long time to fix your cable TV. Isn't your new picture wonderful? We are so happy to be able to offer you this conversion at no charge.*

If you are a teacher who deals with parents, principals, staff, and students, thinking on your feet saves time and sometimes a great deal of hassle:

> *I agree with you, Mrs. Smith. We should both be curious why Andrea didn't bring the sex-education film notice home to you for a signature. Perhaps she can tell us what happened to it.*

Hunting for a job? Responding to interview questions beautifully is part of thinking on your feet (even if you're seated!) Imagine how much better you will feel when you realize that you never again have to respond to a question with a *No.* Instead of having to say, *No, I don't know how to run an XR-7,* you can turn this potential negative into a positive response, with enthusiasm: *I have used the XR-6 and I'm eager to learn the XR-7.*

You can also be confident that your pertinent background information gets out during the interview. And you can guide or control a poor interview. See chapter thirteen for a full discussion of job interviewing.

As a supervisor or manager, thinking on your feet will enable you to deflect hostile questions from subordinates, turning a potential conflict into a workable solution. The result: happier employees and a more harmonious work environment. How are your employee relations? Are you remembering to use those One-Minute Manager type compliments, or do you think of them after you've gone back to your office? That's too late. The techniques of thinking on your feet will help you share the special words at the right moment.

Do you tend to fly off the handle at people, wishing only a few minutes (or even seconds) later that you could take back what you blurted out, undo what you just did? When you can think on your feet you will be less likely to have one of them in your mouth frequently.

As a consumer do you get so irritated that you could scream? Don't you want to be able to make that "perfect" rejoinder–the one which comes to mind just after you get back in the car or hang up the phone? Learn to think on your feet and those great responses will come at the appropriate time, not later. It's hard to call someone later and declare *THIS is what I wanted to say: "Fix it first, and don't call me again until it's right!"*

Are you frustrated when people ask you a question but seem to quit listening before you get it answered? Thinking on your feet will help you get the attention you want for your responses and comments. See chapter fourteen.

In fact, you need to think on your feet if you deal one-to-one with other human beings. Do you want more effective communications with those individuals? Do you want better relationships with them? Do you want to be poised and professional? These are the three attainable goals for people who think on their feet. Discover many more application to your own life as you read examples and practice the techniques here.

The TO DO List:

Before you go on to chapter three, jot down the main reasons you want to think better on your feet. Write down several situations in which better responses will make you happier.

3

About Questions

The first lesson is about questions. The more you know about questions the easier it will be to answer questions posed to you. You will likely know more about questions than most people who query you. If you are asked an appropriate question in the right pattern, you are fortunate. But when asked a question any old way, you will be able to substitute the appropriate pattern as part of your answer (see chapter five). Additionally, you too ask questions as part of your daily life, at work and at home. Using the appropriate question type will help you get better responses from others.

Four basic patterns form most of the questions people ask:

- yes-no questions
- closed information questions
- open information questions
- open-ended questions.

The patterns move from structured or closed (yes-no questions) to unstructured or open (open-ended questions). At the structured end of the spectrum, questions seek information and facts; at the unstructured end, they seek opinions, feelings, or observations.

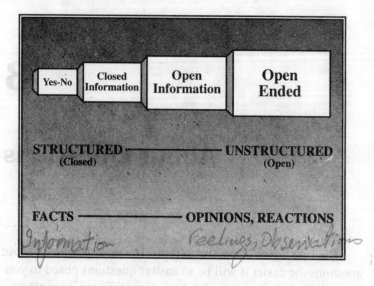

Yes-No Question Patterns

The yes-no pattern creates a question which requests a direct response. These are examples of yes-no questions:

- Are you happy?
- Is this the only color that the suit comes in?
- Did you finish my repairs?
- Was the part ordered the day I called?
- Do you have any houses for sale for under $80,000?
- Was our service satisfactory?

These questions begin with different forms (or tenses) of the verbs *to be, to have, to do,* and words such as *can, would, should,* and *will.*

Yes-no questions are the most used type of question. And because the answer can be a simple *yes* or *no*, that seems like an effective pattern to use, and sometimes it is. This pattern is suited for those instances when you need direct or specific information and you are fairly certain the individual can give it.

Yes-no questions have a definite function in business and personal relationships. These direct questions are useful for taking care of routine details. They are suited for those instances when you need specific information and don't need to build rapport or further a relationship. Yes-no questions are efficient in terms of time—a source of pleasure for busy people.

Problems With Yes-No Questions

Several problems exist with yes-no questions, however. These questions are called closed questions because they often "close" or end the dialogue between two people (see below.) Another problem is that people are seldom satisfied with just a *yes* or *no*; they want/need/desire more information. The result is that the initial yes-no question is wasted, because a follow-up question is required. Choosing an information question instead can usually get both the yes or no and the supporting information at the same time.

A second difficulty is that questioners feel hurt when they receive the simple brusque or terse answers they themselves requested. It is difficult to put much expression or warmth into a one syllable answer. Witness this unfortunate exchange between an automobile owner and a service department employee:

John: *Good morning, Is my car ready?*
Nancy: *No.*
John: (a bit peeved): *Well, when will it be ready?*
Nancy (now also a bit peeved): *It was scheduled for 4:00,*
    so I assume it will be ready by then.

The yes-no question caused unnecessary tension to be created in what ought to be a simple positive exchange:

John: *Good morning. My car is scheduled to be done at*
    4:00. I wonder if it just might be done early.
Nancy: *It will be ready as scheduled, I'm sure. Would*

you like me to call you if it gets done before 4:00?
John: *Yes, thanks, that would be nice.*

Even though it is the not the task of the auto owner to provide good service by being polite, he can make life easier for both of them with a better question. And even though the service provider is supposed to be polite at all times, no one is.

The Communications Contract

The most important difficulty with yes-no questions and answers is that you have cut off, or closed, the conversation. Successful communication—any conversation, social or business—involves an unspoken contract between the participating parties. This contract has two conditions: 1) both people want the communication to succeed, and 2) both people contribute to the communication. The result is a layering effect, a building of the information pool. Each listens and then adds to what the other has said. If either one does not want the conversation to succeed, all that person has to do is not add additional information, and the conversation will soon cease.

To illustrate this contract, notice what happens in the ritual social greeting:

John: *Hi, Nancy.*
Nancy: *Hello, John.*

If neither party contributes beyond the ritual, the conversation is over. But consider this exchange:

John: *Hi, Nancy, how are you?*
Nancy: *John, hi. It's good to see you. I'm fine. I love this sunny weather!*
John: *Me too, I'm planning to go hiking in the Gorge this weekend. Do you hike?*

This building of information not only adds to the knowledge of each person, it also keeps the conversation going smoothly. If you are a sales representative, consider how much rapport-building you have done with just two lines of conversation.

Closed Information Questions

Words such as *when, where, who,* and *what time* seek information by directing the responder and the response to a specific area: *What time may we deliver your supplies? Who will sign for the delivery? What kind of system do you use?*

The response is apt to be as direct as the question: *Friday after 4:00 would be perfect. The purchasing manager. A Zitox 204.*

When the precise information is the only goal, use this question pattern. It too communicates exactly and saves time.

Because the answer can often be just one word, closed information questions can be almost as final as yes-no questions:

Rob: *Where is the meeting?*
Jim: *My house.*
Rob: *Who is attending?*
Jim: *Just about everyone.*
Rob: *When is it?*
Jim: *Tomorrow.*

Not much of a conversation being built here. No rapport is developed. The seeker may get a strong feeling that the responder is not enjoying the conversation. Unless just information is required, these close the conversation and make rapport building difficult. Most of our conversational exchanges seek a bit more than just the answer. But not a speech. See chapter fourteen for problems some people (read women, generally) have by providing more than "just a bit" of extra information.

As a general rule, use the closed information pattern 1) when you are in a hurry and so is the other person; 2) when the conversation is with a person whom you know well, so rapport or goodwill need not be built. Avoid asking this type of question early in an interview or in a conversation with an new acquaintance or client, when the short responses might cut off the discussion too early. Avoid asking these blunt questions when the customer or responder seems intimidated, because this type of question can sound like an interrogation.

Open Information Questions

By contrast the open-information questions–*how, why,* and *what*–are the major open-information question openers, because each typically requires several words to answer them. Responders are encouraged to be open in their responses, to share more information than might be strictly necessary. Consider:

Alfred: *What is the theme of the meeting?*
Valerie: *It's "Safety Pays," the national convention's theme this year.*
Alfred: *How can I help with the meeting?*
Valerie: *You could bring the manuals with you. That would be a big help.*
Alfred: *Why are you hosting it at your house?*
Valerie: *We want a relaxed environment so people won't feel threatened.*

The important information is exchanged. The bonus is rapport building, as warmth and concern are expressed.

Open-information questions are formed with opening words which present larger areas for discussion while still providing some structure. Phrases can also open up the communications and maintain structure: *What about benefits?* or *How about the communications system?* or *How do you feel about the goals?*

These encourage longer responses and more information within a prescribed area of concern.

Open-Ended Questions

These unstructured beginnings are often not questions at all, but invitations. The result is the same: 1) the responder is requested to think through an answer and deliver it at some length; 2) the responder is given latitude to begin wherever he feels most comfortable, has the strongest feelings, or feels most secure. Words to use to get these open responses include *Tell me about...*, *Describe...*, *why* and *how*, when not focused. Examples would be *How are you feeling about this?* or *Why did this happen?*

Open-ended questions are the most indirect. They are designed to encourage people to think, to express opinions, to share ideas. They indicate your wish for such an open response.

Beyond that, the open-ended question encourages a fuller disclosure of information, background, or apprehensions than a typical series of "get those facts first" questions does. So if you are a sales clerk, an outside sales rep or anyone dealing with another human being with whom you wish to establish some rapport, the open-ended question pattern allows that to happen naturally.

Most people need time to open up a bit, to search around for the words. That's basically what this book is about. Those who use open-ended questions thoughtfully recognize people's occasional need to find a comfort level before becoming direct and specific.

When interviewing a potential customer, instead of starting out with "filling out the form" questions, try this:

> *To begin, why don't you tell me about the kinds of services you offer and the needs you see.*

or

First, would you describe your basic business operations?

These open-ended questions establish a comfort level which enables both of you to subsequently deal more directly and completely. It's true that the open-ended approach seems to take longer. But the overall gain in customer-supplier rapport, for example, far outweighs the slight additional time commitment. With an open-ended beginning, you tell a client that she is important as a person and not just as a sale or an account number.

What comes from openness, of course, is much more than just the information you ask for. You gain insight into people's beliefs, their habits, their skills at communications, their detail levels–all good to know in establishing a satisfactory long-term relationship. The more unstructured the question, the more information you are likely to gain.

The unstructured patterns are also used for less precise, but often more important, reactions, feelings, or opinions. When your goal is to determine how someone feels, to discover what is on someone's mind, asking a specific question seldom allows you to discover that. Impatient managers and supervisors rush to judgement with an abrupt *Who let this happen?* or *How in the #@%&**& did this happen?* They minimize their chance of getting a picture of an entire event or a grasp of the extenuating circumstances.

Unstructured questions provide an opportunity to draw people more actively into a conversation. Remember this pattern when you're attending a networking function, or a business meeting.

As you answer questions, remember the goal of each of these patterns. If asked a yes-no question, on most occasions give more of an answer than is requested. However, if you wish not to enter into the communications contract, send a signal that says, *I don't want to have a conversation with you,* by responding briefly.

If people seek precise facts with a closed information question, offer the requested facts and stop, as long as your assessment of the situation indicates no need to build rapport or goodwill.

When asked an open question, give a fuller response, but do not consider it an invitation to tell all you know on the subject. See chapter eleven for tips to guide you in how long you can safely respond to open-ended queries. See chapter fourteen for more on the gender application of longer answers.

4

About Answers ...and Responses

People tend to give answers in one of two common ways: too long and too short. A "too short" answer makes the seeker interrogate you to get all the information that is needed. A "too long" answer (more common) turns out to be a small speech. Chances are, if people wanted a speech, they would have asked you for one.

What's the solution? A response: the answer, plus one piece of support. The support may be a reason, a justification, a statistic, a quotation, a fact, an opinion. Of course you often have many points of support; the secret is to mention just one.

How Much Information Should Be Given?

People are often satisfied with the answer. But they like to hear some depth, some justification, and you should supply it. But what do you do instead? If you are a short answer person, you say *Yes, usually,* or *Sometimes that's true;* or *At 6:00 p.m.,* and then close your mouth. The seeker must ask follow-up questions. Consider this exchange between a club member and a professional speaker:

Marcia: *Do you offer a special discount for nonprofit*

> groups?
> Chelsea: *Yes, usually.*
> Marcia: *Well, would we be eligible for it?*
> Chelsea: *You might be. It depends.*
> Marcia: *What does it depend on?*
> Chelsea: *It depends on several things.*
> Marcia: *Could you give me an example?*
> Chelsea: *Who all you are going to invite, for one thing.*
> Marcia: *Only our members are invited. No outsiders or spouses.*
> Chelsea: *Then you would be eligible for a discount.*

That's a frustrating conversation. The seeker's tone is apt to become irritated because of the shortness of the answers, even though she is partly to blame because of the yes-no pattern she chose. The responder will begin to feel as if she is being interrogated and become hostile, even though she is a big part of the difficulty with short answers and lack of supporting information. She is making the seeker pull the information out of her.

Compare that terse sounding exchange with this one:

> Marcia: *Do you offer a special discount for nonprofit groups?*
> Chelsea: *Yes, I am able to offer one to certain groups. If the audience is solely members, where there is no commercial gain or profit involved, a discount is possible.*
> Marcia: *Wonderful! We do qualify, then.*

The contrast is striking. Three exchanges instead of ten save a great deal of time. Even though the seeker uses a yes-no question, the responder answers more fully. The seeker is pleased with the information she receives; the responder's tone of voice is undoubtedly better: she is conveying positive news in a positive manner. A successful booking is likely.

Building in a Clue

It's easy to suggest giving only one main piece of support. But what if you have lots more wonderful information that you are just dying to give? The suggestion is the same: Give just one main piece of support, but build in a clue which indicates you have more details, if the seeker wishes to hear them.

Remember the premise at the beginning of this chapter, that most people tend to give a small speech when asked a question. We do that for several reasons: We like the sound of our own voice, we are enthused about the topic, we have lots of information to share. None of these reasons is a good reason for telling the seeker lots more than she wants to know.

Building in a clue enables you to respond specifically but briefly, letting the seeker know you will gladly provide more information if she asks a follow-up question. You also build the conversation this way.

Words such as main, *primary, most essential, major* provide the clue: *The main reasons for the change... , The most important factor in our decision... , The primary goal...* The seeker merely says *What are some of the other reasons?* or *What else figured into your decision?* You add more information and you add it confidently because the seeker wishes it. You are not worried about being a bore or losing the seeker's attention. You maintain your credibility, your poise, and your professional demeanor.

Often, though, the seeker will be satisfied with the answer and the main reason. The result is a question and a response, an exchange, with no time wasted and no fear of boring another with excess enthusiasm or information. The communication exchange is successful; the relationship stays positive.

The Basic Communications Exchange

Another, more compelling, reason to give a response with a follow-up clue centers on the nature of the basic communications exchange discussed in chapter three: the contract between two people which requires both to want the conversation to continue and to add information to it. If you respond to a question with five minutes of your great knowledge, wisdom, or opinion, the other person–the other half of your conversation–is left out. He is waiting, patiently or not, for you to draw a breath so he can get back into the conversation.

In other words yours is a monologue rather than a dialogue with the other individual. The exchange of information brought out by a question, a response, a comment and another question, and a response is a natural exchange. Both people are participating, contributing to an ongoing communication process. Both the seeker and the responder are involved; but the seeker won't be involved for long if you give a speech or a monologue.

The question and answer format has turned into a conversation. Whether you are selling, buying, offering service, or asking for service, a conversation will nearly always make a more successful transaction. Rapport is built, confidence grows, and trust begins to be established.

A final reason for including a clue is to remind your brain to stop sending words to your mouth after it sends the main point, the most essential strategy, or the key to success. If you say, *The most important reason we selected this firm is that we know we can work with them,* your brain will understand that it should send no more words down the line. Your brain fulfills the promise of "most important reason" and stops. I have clients, including one real motormouth, who have learned to be concise by mastering and using this one simple tool. It works.

Do You Have to Answer the Question at All?

The answer to that question is "Not necessarily." People answer every question they are asked, just out of habit. Worse yet, some people answer every question exactly the way it was asked. It is not appropriate to do that. Nowhere is it written that you must answer every question asked of you. Shall I remind you that you control what you say? No one forces words out of your mouth.

Even though you can answer, you may not want to answer exactly; you might want to offer only part of the information; or some other piece of information may be more appropriate. As the holder of the information you should decide what to answer and how to answer it. See chapter seven, "Getting a Better Question."

Points to Remember

- To build good relations, have conversations, not question-and-answer periods.
- Give a response: the answer plus one main piece of support.
- Build in a clue to stop yourself from talking too long or to show you welcome a follow-up question.

The TO DO List:

Think about the people with whom you interact on a daily basis. Improve relations with some of those people–at work or at home–by treating them the same way you treat a customer or client.

5

Responding to Easy Questions

How many times have you slapped yourself on the head and exclaimed, *That's what I should have said!* two minutes after you hang up the phone? How often have you thought to yourself, *If only I'd have thought of that earlier?* How frequently do you find yourself muttering, *Why didn't I think of that before?* Realize that the appropriate response was in your mind all the time just waiting to be spoken. But what happened? You blurted out the first thing that got to your tongue, not the best thing you could have said in response.

The secret to responding successfully to all types of questions is easy to remember: Put your brain in gear before you put your mouth in gear. The technique is simple: buy time to think before you talk.

How do you use those precious seconds that you buy? Organize your thoughts. Failure to pause to organize, not first activating your brain, is what causes you to whop yourself in disbelief at what just came out of your mouth. Do you look around to see who else is there? Seems like someone else talking, doesn't it?

With easy questions you can buy enough time to organize just with silence. *Silence?* Yes. Remain silent until your brain has the few second it needs to find the appropriate information. You're dealing with a powerful computing device; your brain needs only a minute amount of time to sort through all your information to get to what you want to utter. The seeker does not expect you to open your mouth the second hers is closed. You generally have four or five times as long to organize as you feel you have before you begin speaking.

What if the time you can naturally buy with silence is not enough time? The other basic time buying strategy is to repeat at least the essence of the question. You can do that in one of two ways: repeat it as a question or repeat it as part of your response. Either way, you can repeat those words easily, giving your brain a few additional seconds to come up with what will follow.

If you repeat the question as a question, nonverbal gestures and intonation are both important. Suppose the question is:

Why have your prices been raised again?

You pause, perhaps nodding slightly, and repeat:

Why have the prices gone up? ... a slight raise was necessary because the cost of paper supplies had doubled in the last six months.

Notice the addition of the word "slight" and the change to the neutral "the price" rather than the personal "your prices." You have diffused the question's negative intention while at the same time answering directly and honestly.

With the identical question, the response which repeats the question as part of the answer is, *It was necessary to raise the prices slightly because the cost of paper had doubled in the last six months.* The negative implication is diffused here too. But don't adopt either approach as your only one. There are many alternative approaches in chapters six-ten.

Don't repeat the question in a rote fashion, like a second grader. Select just the essence. The question is *Do you offer the same type of guarantee for these items you are custom designing and printing as for your stock items that we order?* Your response can be *Our guarantee is valid on all items that we print.*

Don't say *The question is...* unless you are using that phrase to buy yet more time. For more, see below the four reasons to repeat the question.

How Can You Be Successful?

Five basic steps will give you success in responding to all questions:

1. Listen–pay attention to what's already been said
2. Pause to organize
3. Repeat the question
4. Give the one main support (and clue for a follow-up)
5. STOP. Don't end on an excuse.

Listen–Pay Attention to What's Already Been Said

Don't skip over or minimize this vital step, for several reasons. First, you have the opportunity to read the nonverbal messages being sent. These may support the message, but often send a conflicting message to consider. Next, don't feel foolish because you missed some point or repeated what someone else previously said. Third, you can reinforce a key point that someone has made. Fourth, you have the opportunity to correct what you believe to be a misstatement by another. Fifth, you can compliment another by being able to say, *I agree with Joan...* or *Jim's point about that was a good one....* Finally, you can sum up or paraphrase aspects that have been covered, buying more time and improving the total communications situation. And you sound great.

Even if you are conversing with just one person, you can accomplish a great deal more, with more professionalism and confidence, when you know exactly what she said and how she said it–not just parts of it.

(2) Pause to Organize

This essential time-buying phase ensures that you say exactly what you want to say, even with easy questions, rather than only kind of what you want to say. You also look and sound poised and in control when you deliberate for a few seconds, especially if the question is a complex one. There is power in silence.

(3) Repeat the Question

Remember that you can repeat the question two ways, as a question or as part of your answer. If the question is *How long have you been speaking for money, Marian?* my choice of response patterns is 1) *I've been a professional speaker for nearly twenty-five years.* 2) *How long have I been a professional speaker? I got my first paid job twenty-five years ago.*

And notice I rephrased the question slightly to upgrade it. While it's important to repeat the question when speaking with one other person, it is mandatory to repeat it when speaking in front of or with a group. Here are the key four reasons to repeat the question:

...**buys time to think.** It's easy to say the words of the question and your brain is busily searching for what to insert after the question.

...**communicates a complete piece of information.** The answer is only half a piece of information; the question+ the answer is a complete piece.

...**allows you to adjust the question.** You can refocus a hostile or negative question with subtlety. e.g. if the question is *Why are your fees so high?* you could refocus the question slightly in your response, *Fees reflect both my experience and your guarantee of satisfaction.* Or you can clarify the question.

...**enables everyone in the room to hear it**. Whether

you are the speaker, a panel member, or a member of the audience be sure everyone hears the question.

It's frustrating to be in an audience and hear only these three answers from the speaker:

> *Yes, I agree.*
> *I don't think that's applicable in this case.*
> *That's true. I couldn't have phrased it better myself.*

(4) Give the One Main Support

To give a response, not just an answer, add one piece of support to the answer. Most of the time you will satisfy the seeker, enabling him to proceed to the next topic. If you wish to say more, build in the clue word, signaling a follow-up question.

Note: giving one main item of support is a rule of thumb and a reminder to people not to give a speech. You will decide in some situations to give two reasons, or even three. When you give more than one reason, include a frame for your longer response with oral guidelines just as you do in a presentation. This frame is phrased to include the specific number of points you will make: *for these three reasons....* or *here are a couple of considerations: First..., second....*

Here's a complete response with an enumerated frame:

> *Yes, I do support his decision to purchase this system. My opinion is based on three criteria: the cost is within our budget, the quality is high, and the system interfaces with the equipment in the downtown offices.*

A word of caution: most of us have a great deal more information—and tend to give it—than people want. See chapter fourteen for more on this tendency to do a data dump.

Stop–Don't End on an Excuse

This step is vital whether you wish to maintain your professional poise, to appear an assertive consumer, a responsible teacher, or any confident individual. So often people give a fine response, with the right amount of information and the appropriate tone, then blow it all by babbling on beyond the finish or by shrugging at the end. Ask your family or colleagues to monitor whether you have developed one of those two habits. Ask them if you sometimes add a verbal excuse such as *But I don't know if that's what you want you know,* or *But I haven't really studied that aspect yet,* or *I really don't have a strong opinion on that.* If you can't figure out a way to stop, try this trick: repeat the essence of the question as a close: *So that's why we decided to stop the project.* or *And his input is vital.*

Points to Remember:

To respond to questions you wish to answer directly, give your answer, add the main support, and stop. That's all there is to it.

The TO DO List:

Write down three or four basic questions you have to respond to frequently. Practice a response–the answer, plus one main piece of support for each. Also practice building in a clue, to establish a conversation rather than giving a sales pitch.

6

Responding to Difficult Questions

What makes questions difficult to answer? Four categories describe the majority of difficult questions:

- Questions that are long, complex, confusing or not well thought out (chapter seven)
- Questions that are inappropriate to the time and place or questions deliberately designed to intimidate you (chapter eight)
- Questions phrased in a negative way (chapter nine)
- Questions which should be addressed to someone else (chapter ten).

How can you retain the same calm, poised professional or personal demeanor when you've just been thrown a curve? How can you make the seeker feel satisfied? The difficulties and specific solutions are discussed in detail in each of the next four chapters. But first, general tips.

Give a Response, Not an Answer

Use the skills you acquired and practiced in responding to routine questions. Use the same basic tools:

- pay attention and listen carefully
- pause to organize
- repeat the question
- support your answer briefly
- stop.

The new tool is this: give an indirect response instead of a direct one.

To give an indirect response is to answer inductively: give the explanation first, and follow with the answer. The result is a cushioned explanation. To illustrate: If your mate asks you why you are late getting home, your cushioned, indirect response might be

> *After our planning meeting, the boss wanted to talk briefly about my role in the project; she suggested that we go over to The Nest. It was so crowded that we had trouble getting waited on. So what should have been a twenty minute meeting lasted more than an hour.*

Beats "I had a drink with my boss," doesn't it?

Buy Time to Think with Silence

However indirectly you choose to respond, you must still give substance in most instances. So these responses require even more thought and planning than easy responses. The secret is the same: buy time to think. Repeating the question will sometimes do the trick, just as it does with easy questions. Another advantage of repeating the question is that in repeating the words, you're more likely to give the appropriate answer, usually better than just giving the right answer. Assume that you are a management consultant who has just finished making a presentation to the executive committee of a prospective client. You proposed installing an integrated sales/internal-control system that would do a better job of keeping track of the company's inventory. The first question comes directly from the president: *Will this system you are recommending guarantee that we won't have any more shortages in inventory?*

Unless you buy time to think, your candid response is apt to be, *No, I can't guarantee that.* That may be the right answer, but it certainly isn't the appropriate one. Buying some time by repeating the question (and thus hearing it again) should enable you to say

> The question is, "Can I guarantee you'll have no more shortages?" This is, after all, a system, and all systems are fallible. But it is the best inventory system available. I can guarantee that this system will be a tremendous improvement over the way you are now controlling inventory.

Learn to repeat the essence or the intent of the question. This tactic shortens the total response time and focuses the listener on the key element of your response. The next question comes from the vice-president of finance: *You just said that the cost for this fancy integrated system is over $10,000. That's a lot of money. I know there are cheaper systems on the market. I think we don't need such a fancy system.*

Responding to the intent of his comment, you say, *Why do you need to buy the 2000D Series? Because it is by far the best value for the money.* You are also minimizing the negative here. See chapter eight for more ideas on handling negative questions.

Buy Time with a Pause

More often than you realize you can buy enough time to think about what your response will be with silence–just by pausing. Well-timed pauses are powerful, purposeful devices in any oral situation, and responding to questions is no exception. A pause is audio white space, time surrounding a key idea in the same way white space in an advertisement surrounds and emphasizes a key point. A pause also commands attention for what follows in the same way that a colon does in writing when introducing a list.

Finally, a pause prevents fillers such as *uh, er, y'know,* and *and-uh.* These non-words come out of mouths as mental static when brains have not yet become activated. When the brain goes blank it's better to turn off the sound.

Buy Time with a Nonverbal Gesture

A few extra seconds can be gained by a nonverbal gesture. Indicate you've heard the question and you're preparing a response, with a nod, a slight lift of the hand, or a smile (but not ever a grimace.) People who ask difficult questions usually know they are doing so; some will appreciate your thoughtfulness in a measured response. Too, if you begin to speak the instant the seeker closes his mouth, you may sound as if you have a canned answer ready to pull out. People feel that they deserve a personal response. Taking time to think is seen as a compliment; you are saying–nonverbally–"I think your question is a good one, and I'm going to give you a well-thought-out response."

Points to Remember

When asked a question which discomforts you, the basic strategy is the same as with easy questions: buy time to compose your thoughts. Have confidence that the appropriate response will get from your brain to your mouth.

The TO DO List:

Chapters seven-ten involve techniques for difficult questions. Before you read these tips, write down difficult questions you are asked: questions you do not like to answer, questions you should not answer, or questions you cannot answer. Work with your list of difficult questions in the next four chapters.

7

Getting a
Better Question

Often a question is unanswerable because of the kind of question it is: long, winding, complicated, multi-faceted, or obscure. People ask such difficult-to-answer questions for many reasons. Sometimes the seeker simply hasn't thought the question out well enough in advance; the result is a vague question, whether long or short. Don't try to answer a vague question, because you can't please the seeker. Get a better question.

Sometimes the seeker does not know enough about the topic to phrase a question well. This is especially a problem when people seek information about new products or services. Take the opportunity to educate them, by asking an option question, and get a better question to answer at the same time.

Other times, the questioner with lots on her mind tries to get it all into one question; the result is a rambling question with many facets. It's foolish to try to work all the answers into your one response. It's equally foolish to try to figure out which part of the question is most important to the questioner. Get a better question.

Still other times the seeker is trying to stump you, either because he has it in for you or he just likes to sound off–or show off. People who deliberately ask difficult questions believe that complicated question will pin you right to the wall. Don't let that happen. Get a better question.

How Can You Get a Better Question?

Here are five basic ways to get a better question to respond to:

- Ask to have the question repeated
- Ask a question of your own
- Ask for clarification
- Ask for a definition
- Clarify or define a point yourself.

Ask to Have the Question Repeated

The problems with questions, as discussed in chapter three, is that people don't spend much time thinking of how they wish to ask them. That is a big problem when you are attempting to present a poised response. When you ask a seeker to repeat his question, he has a chance to hear it. He is usually glad to repeat it, to have another chance to sound more knowledgeable, less like a dummy. He will frequently begin again with, *What I meant was...,* or *What I was trying to say was....* In most instances you will get a better question to answer. It will typically be shorter, more specific and often more focused. The question is often no longer difficult, but easy.

By the way, if the question does come out exactly the same way the second time, you can be certain that the person is indeed trying to pin you down. His delivery is apt to be more emphatic, more caustic, but the words won't change.

Consider, taxpayer to his state representative at the end of a campaign talk:

You say you're against more taxes. Tell me this, why have you kept voting "Yes" every single time a tax package has come up before the house the last two years that you've been pretending to represent the wishes of this district?

It is important to buy a bit of time to think about your record, so your first response is, *I'm sorry, I couldn't hear all your question; it's a bit noisy in here. Would you repeat it please?*

The taxpayer responds in a pained tone, louder and slower, *I SAID, "You say you're against more taxes... Why have you been voting 'Yes.'..."* You get the idea: word for word, with more emphasis so everyone can hear it this time.

If the taxpayer is seriously asking the question, he is more apt to repeat his question this way: *If you're against more taxes why do you keep voting for more?* Either way, what have you gained? Take as the first assumption that you generally do hear the question; you get the drift. Having it repeated–whether you get a better question or not–buys your brain the additional seconds to figure out what it will send out of your mouth when the repeat is finished. Even if the taxpayer is trying to pin you down, you have a better opportunity to respond with some degree of success than if you have a go at it the first time.

Ask a Question of Your Own

It is nearly always appropriate to ask a question of your own in response to a seeker's inquiry. You are attempting to clarify what the seeker wants to know. This approach is especially important if the question is many-faceted or vague. Do not lost sight of the fact that your goal is more than just giving information; it is successful communication with another person. There is little point to responding with information which the seeker is not seeking. And you lay yourself open to the sarcasm of *Well, that's interesting, but it's not what I asked you,* or *My question was about 1995, not 1996.*

Your goal in asking a question of your own is often to get the seeker to focus the question more, narrow to a more specific time frame, a specific product, a precise problem. And she usually will.

Ask for Clarification

Lack of clarity in an inquiry often means lack of clarity in the questioner's mind. There is little point in your trying to respond brilliantly, because the answer will not please the seeker anyway. He doesn't know what it is he wants. Get a better question by having the seeker clarify to himself and to you what he wants to know. Simply say, *Could you clarify what you mean by "excess"?* or *"Training" is a complex subject; can you be a bit more specific?*

This strategy is a refinement on asking a question of your own, forcing the seeker to do the clarification, not you . A good approach is a choice or option question: *Do you want the figures for 1994 or 1995?* or *Is your concern with the product itself or with the warranty?* or *Do you mean the delivery or the post sale service?* Again, you wish to give the seeker the information he is looking for, if at all possible. Forcing him to clarify the scope of the question will help you do exactly that. Frequently it then becomes an easy question to answer.

Lack of clarity in questions is a problem at home as well as in business. Consider this teenager talking to her parent about restrictions:

Teen: *I don't see why I have to be in at midnight when nobody else does; they can all come home whenever the party is over. It's not easy to get a ride early and I sure don't want you to show up there. I'd be so embarrassed that I'd just die. Why do you have to come?*

Parent: *Well, other kids in your group have curfews too. I was talking to Marcia Jones at the store and she told me that Jason has to be home by midnight. So there'll be other parents there picking up their kids. You shouldn't be embarrassed about having parents. Everybody has parents.*

What a terrible exchange. The teen did not have her real problem identified, and the parent did not help her identify it.

The parent didn't know exactly what the real problem was. If the parent helps her daughter clarify what she wanted to ask, the second part of the conversation could have gone like this:

Parent: *Are you more concerned about the time or about my coming to pick you up?*

Teen: *Well...I guess it's that you'd come up to the door and embarrass me by saying something stupid in front of all my friends.*

Parent: *Let's do this: I'll arrive at midnight and wait in the car for you. If you come out within ten minutes, I won't even need to get out. That will please both of us. OK?*

It's a better exchange. The parent has not nagged her daughter by bringing up a lot of baggage not relevant to the moment. The daughter has said what truly bugs her. Each can feel good rather than bad, and their relationship is improved.

Ask for a Definition

When you are discussing information or concepts which contain words with more than one interpretation, be sure all of you are using those words in the same way. Abstract concepts, projects in the design stage, theories of finance, inventory methods, sales approaches–all these can be defined by the seeker to make certain you and she are using the words the same way. Especially with abstractions and theories, you may confidently expound at some length, only to be greeted at the close of your response with, *What in the world ARE you talking about?*

Your punctured ego will have difficulty getting back to normal size, resulting in your less-than-poised performance for at least the next few exchanges. Avoid potential deflated egos by asking the seeker to define the word which can lead to trouble. It is easy to say, *Could you define "value-added" as you perceive it?* or

Would you give me your definition of "moral" in this context?
You will both be on the same page as you begin your response.
Remember, it is not necessary for you to agree with the definition,
just to understand how the seeker is using the word. If you do
disagree, part of your response may be in defining it yourself.

If the seeker has asked the tough question to put you on the
spot, you are gently but firmly putting her on that spot–all without
a smudge on your poise. If she cannot define the term, which is
sometimes the case with troublemakers, she will probably mumble
something and withdraw. No more difficult question to answer.

If she can and does define it, wonderful. You have two
advantages now: a clearer understanding of how the inquiry is
focused and more time to get your response ready, during the
moments the definition is being readied and spoken.

Clarify or Define a Point Yourself

As the responder you also have the option to clarify the
question as you heard it or to define a concept. Some people
believe they can maintain better control if they clarify by
re-focusing the question in their response. The down side of
clarifying an inquiry yourself is you may not clarify to the
satisfaction of the seeker. Your response is also longer if you do
the clarification or definition. It is easy to run on too long in this
preliminary material and not get to the answer. However, that in
itself can be a successful avoidance tactic. (See chapter eight on
"Redirecting The Question.")

How might this definition process begin your response?

> Stockholder: *It seems to us that you just keep spending
> money. Why are you doing that instead of giving us
> bigger dividends?*
>
> CEO: *If by "spending money" you are referring to the
> new integrated sales/inventory system we installed, I
> am delighted to tell you that the system has improved* ·

our shipment time by 40%, giving us a net increase in profits of 30%. You will see some of that profit increase in your dividends this year.

If you use the clarification approach, consider this exchange:

Parent: *When I look at my kid's class schedule, all I see are educational classes. Why aren't you giving him stuff to help him get a job?*

Principal: *I take the word "educational" to mean classes such as history and English. The core of our curriculum is dictated by the State Board of Education, and certainly those classes are part of that core. But in English class, for example, teachers are including some business letter writing as assignments. Those will help your son get jobs and also do solid work in his profession, whatever it will be.*

Avoid the temptation to let the seeker confirm your clarification with this type of beginning: *By "educational" do you mean history and English?* While this approach may appear helpful to be certain the conversation is on track, the great problem is letting the seeker back into the lead: he may launch into his favorite speech about what's wrong with education, or he may ask yet another question. At minimum he will confuse the issue and give you a more difficult topic to respond to. Get your response to this question out, clearly and with poise, before you are hit with some other onslaught.

Points to Remember

Getting a better question to answer will alleviate many seemingly difficult questions, turning them into easy questions– the kind you can answer and you want to answer.

8

Hedging, but Still in Control

The second category of difficult questions is those which are inappropriate and those with hidden agendas. The solution: Hedge. Some people think hedging has a bad reputation, as if nice people didn't do it. They're not well-informed. Perhaps they're confusing "hedging" with, to use current jargon, blowing smoke. "To hedge" simply means to answer indirectly, or to refuse to commit oneself.

Chapter six discussed basic indirect responses. This indirect approach is especially necessary with questions you could answer but don't want to answer directly. For whatever reason, you decide that it is not appropriate to give the exact information the question seeks. People frequently ask questions that are either inappropriate or–let's be candid here–ignorant (read *ignorant* in its true definition: "showing lack of knowledge.") These folks probably mean well, but they do not realize that their query puts something at risk: confidential information, non-public facts, private estimates, prices. These people are not necessarily at fault; however, the problem remains: sounding poised and credible while not disclosing the confidential information.

Occasionally, you may be tempted to simply say, *That's none of your business.* Resist that temptation, unless you have beautiful control of your voice and intonation. It is possible to say, *This information is classified,* or *Those figures have not been released yet.* Tone of voice is still important with such responses. Be careful to give such a seeker the chance to save face. No one wishes to be embarrassed because of lack of knowledge. If the seeker happens to be someone significant to your work or your life, it is particularly essential to give an appropriate response to that inappropriate question. Such a response is apt to be indirect, or hedged.

There are also people who know very well that the information is privileged. They ask the question anyway; they like to see you squirm. Do the same cautions apply to these jerks? Yes, usually. While it is tempting to put those kind of people down with a witty one-liner, such poor judgement usually comes back to haunt you. That old geezer whom you made the object of your biting sarcasm turns out to be the new majority stockholder. The smart young thing you put in her place with a witty quip is the daughter of your biggest donor. It costs you nothing to remain professional and it might cost you a great deal to lose your cool or give in to a whim.

Tactics for Hedging Professionally

There are four basic approaches to choose from when seeking to respond indirectly in these situations:

- Respond to one aspect of the question
- Refocus the question
- "Discuss" the question
- Build a bridge between the inappropriate question and an appropriate response.

Delivery is the key to success when employing any of these hedging tactics. Poor delivery when responding indirectly causes audiences to be put off. Such need not be the case. Knowing that the indirect approach is the appropriate one should give you confidence to carry it off. See chapter eleven for special tips on delivery.

Respond to One Aspect of the Question

With difficult questions, one common problem is that there are a number of aspects which need to be addressed. In this case the problem becomes the solution: pick the one aspect you wish to speak to and form your response around it. Ignore the rest. If your response has met the criteria discussed earlier, chances are excellent you will have satisfied the seeker. Remember, people ask questions for many reasons other than to get information. They want to hear you talk, to measure your poise, to get your slant, to reassure themselves. A many-faceted question is frequently the result of someone not knowing exactly what to ask, or even exactly what he seeks. A solid, positive response on one aspect, with specific support and delivered with a confident tone, will satisfy many seekers.

What if one solid aspect does not satisfy the seeker? What if he comes back with, *You didn't answer my question: What about the stock options?* Are you hurt? No. You did hear that part too, and your brain probably gave it a bit of attention. So your second response will be better than your first one might have been. You can ask to have that part rephrased, buying yourself even more time to deal with the appropriate material. Consider this exchange between a manager and her secretary:

Secretary: *Last week you said that we could talk about the financial and growth opportunities for me here at XYZ Corp. Please tell me about the training program. Am I eligible for the promotion plan? and what are the*

rumors I hear about the stock options available for
management and not staff?

Boss: *This is a good time to talk about those
opportunities, because I have just finished the new
employee brochure. You are eligible for the training
program now, and for the promotion plan after you
have been here one year. The training agenda will be
available in my office whenever it gets back from the
printer.*

Secretary: *Well, that helps me, but you didn't talk about
the stock options.*

Boss: *What specific question did you have about the stock
options?*

Secretary: *I wondered how it worked and whether I was
eligible.*

Boss: *It's based on a formula of years of service, plus
other variables in salary scale; the professional
training and the promotion plan are designed
exclusively for staff; the stock option is, at this time,
available only for management.*

Notice that the good news is positively presented, the bad
news is down-played in this indirect response. You might say that
it's buried.

Refocus the Question

When a question is directed toward material which is
confidential or simply information you do not wish to share,
refocus on a less restricted aspect. Take one word from the
question (usually not the main topic word) which you are willing
to talk about, and build a strong, supported response around it.

Consider this question from a parent to his son's high school counselor:

> Parent: *I just can't understand why my son isn't doing any better in school. He's got a good mind, he generally does his homework, he doesn't miss classes too often, he tells me, and he gets along ok with most of his teachers. Why is he not passing?*

Examine this question carefully. The counselor does not want to say John has such a rotten attitude that none of the teachers can reach him, that his homework–when done–is sloppy and illegible, and that he's missed enough classes that he's behind in three. The counselor may need to say those things at some point in the conversation. But he will want to deal with them one at a time, after he has built some rapport with this parent. Trying to respond to all of them right at the beginning of a conference would be inappropriate for many reasons: 1) the response becomes a speech because each criticism must be supported; 2) the parent is listening rather than contributing, so no conversation is built; 3) the parent is put on the defensive, having his child attacked; 4) the parent is not having his support enlisted. Here's the entire dialogue, with the counselor's indirect response pattern:

> Parent: *I just can't understand why my son isn't doing any better in school. He's got a good mind, he generally does his homework, he doesn't miss classes too often, he tells me, and he gets along ok with most of his teachers. Why is he not passing?*
>
> Counselor: *John DOES have a good mind, Mr. Jones, and when he wants to use it, he can do work at the higher range of the class. He needs to decide that it's important to use his mind in every class. How do you think you might be able to help him decide to put that fine mind to work more often?*

The counselor's goals are to keep the dialogue going, to avoid having to say all negative things right up front, and to enlist the parent in the solution rather than placing him on the defensive. All of these can be accomplished 1) by buying time to think, so the appropriate thing is said, rather than the "correct" thing; 2) by using an indirect approach, to soften a mostly negative situation; and 3) by employing the strategy of refocusing the question as the pattern for the response.

"Discuss" the Question

People frequently ask what seem like difficult questions, when what they really want is general information. I remember a question and answer session in an audience of Washington and Oregon business people. The person fielding the questions was an assistant in one state's Office of Economic Development. One question was *How come Oregon and Washington don't cooperate more in economic development?*

That sounds like a real zinger. The responder was a pro; his opener was *More cooperation goes on than is apparent.* He mentioned one or two projects, talked about various reasons that it didn't happen more (including competition) and closed with, *But, I've really just discussed your question.* This finish was accompanied by a charming smile.

It was a classic response. Of course he just discussed it, because that was all he could do—that type of question has no answer, and discussion is exactly what the seeker—and the audience—wanted. The better question would have been *Talk about the opportunities and problems of cooperation between our two states.* But as a speaker you don't often get the better question, so you respond to what's asked in the appropriate way. Many times a discussion is that appropriate way.

Delivery counts here too. The responder who is poised and in control has no trouble with the charming smile and warm tone which the end of this kind of response needs.

Build a Bridge

A bridging response is a variation of the refocusing tactic, but more versatile–and more difficult to carry off. Bridging enables you to move from what the seeker asked to what you want to talk about, even if you can't find a key word as your focus. The key here is obvious: the bridge must be strong enough to be a logical transition between the material of the question and your response material. If the bridge is not strong, it sounds faked. A successful bridging response is a beautiful piece of professional speaking; a poor one sticks out for a mile.

The easiest way to construct the bridge is to briefly acknowledge what the seeker said and go on quickly from there. "Where you go" is typically to what you see as the more important aspect of the situation. Here's a bridge:

> Unconvinced prospective client: *I don't know. Your price is substantially above those of your competition. It's not going to be easy for me to convince my board to pay that much more.*
>
> Responder: *You're right that price is important, Jack, but quality is even more important, because you're looking at an investment, not just a purchase. You expect longer product life and you will get it. You expect a refinement of features and this model has them. Quality is the key.*

Another successful bridge:

> Q: *I want to know why we aren't sending more money to the XYZ project. It's a good project.*
>
> A: *Yes, it's a good project. But money's only one issue here. The critical issue is change. We're planning to...*

One more example:

Q: *I'm concerned about the wheat we're shipping to that country. Why are we selling to our adversaries?*
A: *That's certainly one area of concern. But of even greater concern are farmers' grain surpluses; we must...*

You get the idea: agree that something said is valid, true, or of concern, and agree with it if you can. Then move quickly to the greater concern or more important issue you want to talk about.

You may be more familiar with this tactic than any of the others. Listen to the news conferences of elected officials, appointed officials, and candidates for good and not-so-good examples. If the bridge was well built you either won't recognize it, or you will discover it later, when you replay the dialogue in your mind. A poor bridge is easy to spot: people's reaction is apt to be *Give us a break! The question was about Iraq; how did you get to South Africa?*

This tactic requires even more practice than most others. But when handled with a poised, confident style it is a lifesaver, especially for situations when you have an agenda and you must get it covered. It's also helpful for those whose dealings require talking a great deal without giving much away. If you need this kind of response you will see its application to your area of expertise.

Points to Remember

Do not be embarrassed by the need to hedge. It is legitimate for inappropriate questions, and acceptable for questions you cannot answer. Approach hedging with confidence. Check chapter eleven for delivery tips to enhance that confidence.

9

Responding to Negative Questions

A third reason questions are difficult is that people phrase them in a negative way. Avoid repeating either their negative words or negative tone. Your goal is to respond so that the focus of the question itself becomes positive.

Negative questions include words such as *don't, can't, wouldn't, shouldn't*. Consider the parent whose query is *Why can't my son read?* The teacher who can think on her feet simply turns both the question and the response into a positive encounter. This tactic not only defuses an angry parent, it restores goodwill to the conversation and finds a solution to the problem. Here's one such turn-around:

Parent: *Why can't my son read?*
Teacher: *I'm glad that you're concerned about Jack's reading level. One important thing you can do to help him is to read to him at home.*

Another possible response might be

Teacher: *I'm concerned about Jack's reading level too. Reading aloud to him at home would help him develop an interest in books. His skills will improve quickly when he becomes interested.*

When responding, the teacher used three techniques: 1) she repeated the question as part of the answer; 2) she changed the negative concept *can't read* to a neutral *reading level;* 3) she refocused the question, a tip discussed in the preceding chapter.

Why Negative Questions?

People who phrase their questions in negative words are people who had a expectation which was not met. Some are disappointed or hostile. Some are people whose deadline has not been met; they are apt to be customers or clients. Others are people who had a request turned down by someone; these are apt to be subordinates. Identify what the expectation was, then give the seeker an explanation. Avoid increasing their hostility or their disappointment. You can manage this feat simply by remembering not to go along with the either the negative tone or the negative words.

Still other people ask negative questions because, not getting what they wanted, they see no recourse. These include subordinates, students of all ages, and children. Avoid buying into the negative with them too. Consider the high school student whose complaint is, *Why don't I ever get an 'A' on a paper?* The response is too often apt to be *Because you don't follow directions.*

The better response turns the negative to positive, conveying the same answer, while also giving a compliment:

Teacher: *You do know the information. You can earn an 'A' on a paper if you follow the directions of the assignment.*

or

Teacher: *Following the directions of the assignment will get you an 'A' every time if you know the material as well as you knew this material.*

Maybe the question is directed to a parent:

Child: *Why can't I have a computer? Everybody else has one.*

Parent: *You can earn the money to buy a computer by shoveling snow for the neighbors this winter.*

Points to Remember

Negative statement can be phrased positively. Is the glass half full or half empty? It depends on your perspective. Turn the negative to a positive, follow with the answer. Ignore hostility, a whiny tone or guilty dig that accompanies these questions.

10

Getting Someone Else to Respond

The person who receives a question is occasionally not the person best equipped to answer it, especially in a group situation. One of the following three alternatives to redirect the question improves the chances for an excellent response:

- Redirect the question to a colleague if one is present (there are rules which govern this. See below.)
- Redirect the question to another member of the audience, either a specific person (in which case the same rules apply) or to the general audience
- Redirect to the seeker (in certain situations; see below)

Examine the last option first. A difficult question is sometimes made so by the vehement demands of the questioner, who actually is looking for a forum or platform for his views. Sometimes it works best to let him talk–briefly–by asking for those views.

Let a Difficult Listener Speak–Or Not?

Some speakers believe it is never a good idea to give a hostile or difficult person the floor. This thinking suggests that to allow a forum for an opposing idea will cause your own performance to be less than successful. There certainly are instances where that is true. This approach is risky if you are not sure that you can regain control.

Consider the positive possibilities first. In certain gatherings, especially in-house meetings, such people will be heard. If you don't give them a forum, they will find one after the meeting, in the newspaper, on television, or on the internet. In meetings of the board, the stockholders, the faculty, or the staff, it is impossible to keep those people bottled up. And odds are that you shouldn't leave them bottled up, even if you are the Chair or the President who could ignore them if you exercised your power.

Think of this scenario the same way you think of "overcoming objections" in sales. It's better to discover and overcome as many objections as you can. The objections are there, whether you elicit them and discuss them—or not. If you don't get them handled, they will still come out. The problem is obvious: when you are not there, who knows what kind of wild rumors and misinformation will be bandied about? Deal with them. And keep control.

The same is true, exactly, with the kinds of questions that people ask which have angry exclamation points at the end instead of question marks. Those grumbling malcontents will talk to anybody they can; you are far better off to let them have their brief moment. The operative word is brief: let them speak briefly, respond briefly and then move swiftly to the next question or the next agenda item. This action gets that problem behind you, instead of out there roaming around, causing discontent to grow.

The key to control is eye contact. Look directly at the person in a firm or commanding manner and request his input. Here's some language to use: *John, those views need to be expressed. We want to consider all side of the issue. Our agenda is tight today, but let me give you a couple of minutes to air them.* As soon as he begins speaking, **take your eye contact away from him.** He will usually run down quickly, when you aren't watching his performance. After the two minutes are up, signal a finish, or interrupt firmly with

Thanks, John, for that input. Next item.... If the material needs discussion, or a vote, dispatch it firmly. Note: modify these instructions depending on who the individual is and what your company politics requires.

Those grumblers also make snide comments to their neighbors, whispering in a voice loud enough to be heard, without asking a public question. My advice to clients who face such situations is to diffuse such disruptions by drawing attention to them, not the reverse. It's your board meeting; you believe that the young gun from the downstate office will once again badmouth much of what is being discussed. You are of course standing as you chair the meeting; you are moving around as you write on the whiteboard, make your points, facilitate discussion. Draw attention to him by being near him. Because you are moving around, it's easy to move smoothly and casually over to where that person sits. If you're inside a U-shaped arrangement, stroll over to stand directly in front of this malcontent. Lean slightly against the table, your back to him, or place your hand on the table. Alternately, you're moving around the outside of a large conference table. Stroll around as you talk, or listen. Stand behind this person. In some instances, place your hand lightly on the back of his chair; in an extreme moment, rest your hand lightly on his shoulder, as you pass. It works.

Not an In-house Situation?

If you have a public speaking situation, not an in-house one, a judgement must be made each time. Consider these facets: who you are; what your relationship is to the group; whether you are ultimately accountable to them; whether you can be helped more than hurt by dealing with opposition rather than ignoring it.

In situations where you have decided to let that person speak, giving her a brief platform from which to expound, use the same strategy as described above: firm eye contact given and then withdrawn, and the same type of language in your comment. Though you are not looking at her, be listening carefully so you 'can pull out one aspect you wish to respond to, one point you wish to make. Close off the encounter with your strong remarks. Your comment might be *It is good to have those views expressed; the key concern for all of us is _____.* or try *Thank you for expressing your point of view; you and I agree that _____, and that will be our focus this year.* You are using the strategy "speak to one aspect," (chapter eight) or "respond positively to a negative question" (chapter nine). Deliver this brief line strongly, and then turn to another part of the audience with *Next question?* Your words and eye contact strategy enable you to put that person in a box. Don't open it again: don't give that person eye contact again.

And if you prefer not to give that person the opportunity to speak? Ask him instead to rephrase the comment into a question with language such as this: *What exactly is your question?* or *Could you please rephrase that into a question?* Once you get a specific question, use one of the many strategies in these chapters. Look directly at the seeker as you begin your response; but withdraw it, and don't give this individual further eye contact. After you have finished your response, turn firmly to the other side of the room with *Next question?* or the next agenda item.

Redirect the Question

You are part of a team presentation or a panel. The question, though addressed to you, is in the area of expertise of some other panel member. You should redirect the question to that individual, but only if you follow the precise rules of redirecting. On occasion a member of the audience is the expert; you imagine he is willing, even eager, to respond. Should you redirect the question to him? Yes, but only if you follow the rules.

The Rules for Redirecting

The rules for redirecting the question to another person, either one of your colleagues or someone in the audience, embody the

Golden Rule for responders: "Do unto others as you would have them do unto you." There are four aspects:

1. **Get the attention of the person to whom you are redirecting.** Begin by saying her name loudly and clearly, so she is alert to what is about to happen.
2. **Repeat the question clearly.** She may not have heard the question.
3. **Buy her some time.** Give explanation about her expert background. You're also justifying why you aren't answering it. Even if she isn't more qualified, extra time will help her respond better than you could.
4. **Identify the seeker,** if possible.

Between a client and a stockbroker, it might go something like this:

Client: *Why have commodities margins been going down so much lately?*

Stockbroker: *Jane Jones of our Portland office specializes in commodities; she could give a clear picture of why the margins have been decreasing in the last few months. In fact, she has made a special study of commodities margin recently. Jane, could you respond to Mr. Jackson's query about commodities margins?*

Woe unto you if you miss a step. You can be exiled to a branch office for dropping a question on an unprepared and unsuspecting someone.

Someone who secretly wishes to be friendless at work might respond in this manner: *Gosh, that's a tough question to answer; we'll ask our specialist. What do you think, Jane?*

How would you like to have that dumped in your lap? We have all been guilty of dropping such a bomb. In a team situation, the strength of one member equals the strength of the entire team, so if Jane looks or sounds foolish, you all do. And there goes the project you were bidding on.

What about asking someone from the audience to respond? Your judgement is needed here each time. Base your judgement on these criteria:

- **Who is the audience?** If you are peers or equals, you can pass along a question.
- **What is the purpose of the gathering?** If its overall purpose is a collective growth in professional knowledge, you can pass it on.
- **Who am I in relation to the audience?** If you are there as the authority, the guru, it's best not to pass it on. However, if you are first among equals, passing it on is a compliment, provided that you follow the rules for redirecting and don't embarrass someone.

Points to Remember:

Redirecting the question can strengthen a team. It can also be a gesture of good will or a compliment. Examine the gathering, determine your options, and share the spotlight when you can. Delivery counts; redirect the question with a confident tone and a strong presence. Otherwise you appear unprepared.

With hostile listeners, allow comments but keep control. Your image will be strengthened as a person not threatened by opposing views. Delivery counts here too. Read the next chapter carefully.

The TO DO List:

Make a list of situations and places where you speak, regularly or occasionally. Beside each, note instances when you should allow an antagonist to speak his piece.

11

Delivery–the Secret to Success

What counts, finally, is often not so much what you say as how you say it. People ask questions for many reasons other than just seeking information. They are trying to find out about you. The tremendous amount of information that you communicate about yourself nonverbally is reflected in your delivery. Many people give mediocre responses with superb delivery; they generally fare better than those with good responses and mediocre delivery skills. Your personal goal is both good response and good delivery.

Your overall strategy is to respond from a position of strength and credibility, not from a position of weakness and vulnerability. You demonstrate this confident position with your delivery.

Tips on Delivery

Strategic pauses, a strong voice, vocal emphasis on key words, voice variety–these four delivery skills augment the direct responses and enhance the indirect ones as well. Practice tone, pauses, and vocal emphasis.

To begin, pick a simple sentence such as "He said he loves my sister." Each time you repeat it, put emphasis on a different word: "He *said* he loves my sister." "He said *he* loves my sister."

"He said he *loves* my sister." "He said he loves *my* sister." and, "He said he loves my *sister.*"

What happens? The meaning changes each time you emphasize a different word. This simple tool improves your vocal emphasis of key words. Practice other sentences, changing meaning with just your voice.

Practice when driving alone in the car. After a few tries out loud, you will quit feeling foolish. Be as extreme as you want to be, in varying your tone and emphasis. You will hear improvement almost immediately. Keep practicing. Learn the power of your voice, and use it.

Basic theory about pauses was discussed in chapter six: pauses are one key to thinking before you speak. Pauses are also powerful delivery tools. Use pauses both to emphasize what you have just said and to prepare the listener for an upcoming strong idea. Pauses are useful to let the words sink in to the seeker's mind. Pauses slow your mind down to search for the exact word, not just any word.

Eye Contact Counts

Effective eye contact is important in all successful communications; in responding to questions it becomes even more important. When responding to difficult questions from a group, it is vital. One person asks the question, but it is usually on the minds of several. Your responsibility is to the group, not just to the seeker. Let your eyes slowly move from person to person as you repeat the question. Give the seeker quick eye contact at the beginning of the actual response, then look at others throughout the rest of the response. It is a good practice to return eye contact to the seeker just as you finish. Two problems make that strategy difficult to accomplish, however: first, timing is difficult; second and much more important, the seeker sees this as an invitation to ask another question. Since the goal of a question and answer session is to get as many people involved as possible, you generally don't take more than one question from anyone except the decision-maker.

Responses That Require Superb Delivery

Two other response options exist that depend for their success almost entirely on your delivery:

- the candidness of admitting you do not know or do not have the information
- meeting a tough question head on that you can answer but would prefer not to answer directly.

To remain on top of a situation and keep everyone's confidence, both of these options require superb delivery. Both options will gain you new respect from friend and foe alike.

I don't know, but...

Often the best response is the candid one: *I don't know....* What too often happens, though, is that people feel they should know, so they try to fake it. They fumble around in an attempt to cover the lack of knowledge; everybody can tell. Or else they blush, giggle, or get embarrassed. Never mind what you should know. Most of the time people don't care if *you* know it; they just want the information. Don't try to fake it. Fumbling around puts everything you have already said in jeopardy. Down goes your credibility not to mention your confidence. The goal, as with any difficult question, is to project an overall sense of poise.

For example, if a sales representative is asked the specifications of a certain product, his response may be a firm, positive *I don't know... but let me call you later on this morning with those figures.* Notice the specific commitment to get the information to the seeker.

Another response might be, *I don't have those figures in my head. Let me check the drawings and get right back to you.* Or consider this response: *I want to give you the precise numbers; let me double check them and call you this afternoon.* Use this one only if you do have a rough idea, though, because the seeker is apt to say that the numbers don't have to be precise.

Try this approach: *That's a new product and I haven't yet committed the numbers to memory. Will you be in your office after lunch? I'll call you with them.* Speak with no tinge of embarrassment or lack of confidence. Then make a commitment, generally the more specific the better, to get the information to that person. In a speaking situation, say *Give me your card after the session, so I can get the information to you.*

Even better, though, is to just **think** the words *I don't know, but...* opening your mouth to speak when you get to the action you promise to take. Say *let me call you about those figures right after this meeting,* or *I can find out the exact amount with one quick phone call. Stay right here.* This strategy takes practice, but in time you will find it easy to speak with confidence even when you don't know an answer.

The Direct Approach to a Tough Question

Some tough questions need to be tackled straight on. This approach is impressive and refreshing, especially for politicians, bureaucrats, and management. The individual who can respond forthrightly gets some additional points for credibility from her audience and even from her antagonists and opponents. Delivery is the total key here; in fact, if you are good enough at delivering words, you may not need most of this book. An honest tone and well-timed pauses are essential. Consider this exchange between a political candidate and a taxpayer:

Taxpayer: *Will taxes go up if we approve this addition to the highway system?*

Candidate: *Taxes **will** go up. [pause] When we compare the 3 percent per thousand increase with the cost of automobile repairs caused by these poorly surfaced roads, people will find that their overall cash-out-of-pocket will be less because automobile repairs should go down significantly.*

Notice the emphasis on *will*; notice the pause after the affirmative statement to let the message sink in. No *but* or *however* signals what the audience will feel is another excuse. This is explanation, not an excuse.

Here's an exchange between a CEO and a stockholder:

Stockholder: *I heard that our dividends will be less this year. Is that true?*

CEO: *It **is** true. [pause] The economy is still depressed, the sales have not yet regained their momentum, and the results are that profits are down across the board.*

The order of the words varies in this direct approach. The information is the same as with an indirect approach; the difference is the answer, the bad news, is up front. Make sure that you are able to give these direct responses to bad news questions when you need to. Practice your delivery.

Responding to Open-ended Questions

Delivery tips should also include a primer in reading the nonverbal clues of the seeker. These clues are particularly important when you are asked an open-ended question you believe is deliberately asked: the seeker wants a full response. Three such instances are job interviews, when meeting a superior for the first time, and in an evaluation interview. The question should be an open *Tell me about yourself,* or *Describe how you felt about that,* or *Tell me about your experiences with* _____

Seekers will communicate nonverbally how long you should talk. They will signal you to keep talking in one of two basic ways. One is head nodding as you enthusiastically describe your feelings. The other is a soft, low volume expression such as *I see* or *Hmmm* or *OK.* The key is the low volume. Though you can hear it, it is not loud enough to be an interference. Both these messages signal "Keep talking."

However, if the *I see* or *OK* is delivered at normal, or higher, volume, the seeker is indicating he has heard enough. You must stop. An interviewer can also nonverbally signal a stop by looking back at your resume, picking up your evaluation sheet, or turning back to the desk. Stop as soon as you can.

Sometimes, especially in casual conversation, people do not signal; their eyes just glaze over. This message is harder to pick up because we are usually so involved in our own enthusiasm that we do not notice the eyes as quickly as we should. Remember the concept of the contract that two people make to communicate successfully. For a dialogue to develop, both need to contribute. If you go on at length, even with an open-ended question, you are giving a monologue. See chapter fourteen for more on talking beyond your listener's interest.

So, thinking on your feet also means not responding at length every time you are asked an open-end question. Remember how you feel when in a weak moment you ask someone how his recent operation went.

Points to Remember:

- Good delivery techniques:
- Absolute confidence in your tone
- Special emphasis on key words
- Effective use of pauses
- Careful eye contact

These techniques are particularly necessary when responding *I don't know...* and when answering a tough question straight on.

The TO DO List:

Jot down two or three responses to questions people ask you which in the past you have answered *I don't know.*

12

Buying Time
Over the Telephone

When the seeker with a difficult question cannot see you, a variety of tactics can help you to move the communications along, while keeping you in control. The secret once again is successful delivery of the tactic. When asked a question on the telephone that you would like time to frame the most appropriate response to, find a way to either return the call or get the caller to hold. Here's how:

I'm in a colleague's office; let me get back to my desk.

or

I picked up this call in the conference room; may I call you right back?

or

John, you've caught me in a meeting; are you in your office? I'll get right back to you with those numbers.

or

My secretary has that folder on his desk; hold just a second and I'll get it. I want to give you the exact numbers, not an estimate.

You get the idea. The caller does not know the actual situation and he usually doesn't care. He simply wants the information. You buy seconds or minutes to look at the numbers, phrase the appropriate response, then pick up the telephone again. Be sure to commit to a specific time to get back to the seeker. This strategy works well provided your tone is confident and poised; you will sound foolish only if your delivery is stumbling or hesitant.

Are you fibbing? Not at all. Your ultimate goals, remember, are 1) effective communication of the required information; 2) good client, management, or personal relations; 3) credibility. You achieve those three goals by being in control of your portion of the communication and by relaying the information in a manner that best meets the requirements of the relationship.

If you are actually in the conference room or a colleague's office, this response would be automatic. Learn to make it equally automatic whenever you need to buy time to think. If you need the strategy frequently, don't get a videotelephone.

13

The Job Interview

Use the same tools and strategies to respond to questions during a job interview:

- listen fully to the question
- buy time to think with a pause
- repeat the question as part of your answer (See pg. 40 for a summary of reasons to repeat the question.)

You will shine. Buying time to think gives you the opportunity to give the appropriate response, not just the first answer that pops into your mind. You can also help guide the interview. Eager job candidates mistakenly think the interviewer is in control of the interview. But you can do a great deal to control the flow, the pace and even the questions, if you are prepared to.

Why be prepared to control the interview? Because not all interviewers are equal; they come in all types: some are experienced and skilled; others are novices; still others are tired, ill, or lazy. If you get an interviewer from any category but the first, be prepared to make things happen yourself. Your goal in an interview is to present a complete picture of yourself. By guiding the interview you can be certain the picture is complete, no matter what type of interview, or interviewer, you get.

Guiding or Controlling the Interview

Learn two ways to guide or control an interview: First, through preparation, know what information you must communicate to paint that complete picture (plus additional information which will enhance that picture, if time and circumstances allow); second, use each question to include a portion of that information, regardless of how much information the question seeks. Remember, you don't have to respond to a question just the way it's posed. Sometimes you want to adjust the question (see chapters seven and eight). You can answer with less or–probably–more information than is sought.

How Much Information Should You Give?

How much should you say? The type of question is the first clue: open questions encourage fuller responses; closed questions request conciseness (see chapter three). In spite of those general guidelines, if you want to give more–or less–information on a particular topic, you can. You control what comes out of your mouth. If it is a closed factual information question, *How many accounting software packages do you know?* you may answer concisely, *I've used three - Peachtree, AccPac, and MAS90.* But if accounting software is a strength of yours, use a longer response to develop that strength:

Competence with a accounting software is one of my strongest areas. I've taken classes in three – Peachtree, AccPac, and MAS90. My last two jobs gave me in depth experience with AccPac and MAS90. I discovered that knowing one package makes it a simple task to pick up others. Because accounting terms are standard and results are uniform, learning how to get a program to generate any particular report, for example, is easy for me.

They emphasised on thorough Pdt. knowledge & how to match that of the need of the customer. So it was like a puzzle. Matching needs w/ I'm confident that I can learn your pdts quickly.

Pdts. and I loved solving that puzzle.

THE JOB INTERVIEW   **87**

Even if the question is an open-ended one, such as *Tell me about your familiarity with accounting software*, your goal is to give an initial response that is concise. In such cases, you may choose to discover what direction the interviewer wants you to go. Ask a choice question as your response (see chapter seven): *Yes, I'd be glad to. Would you like to hear first about my training or my experience?* The choice question forces the interviewer to select a direction. However, if you'd like to set the direction, choose either the aspect that is your strength or the aspect which hasn't yet been covered.

> *My* **training** *in accounting software is extensive. I've had courses in MAS90 and AccPac, with two years of hands-on lab. I also learned the accounting package for Peachtree while an intern at CCC Corporation.*

or

> *As I mentioned earlier, I've had lots of training in accounting software; I've also used two of the three packages in a work situation. My internship at CCC Corporation used Peachtree and my summer accounting work in the business office at the community college was with AccPac.*

What if you need to answer briefly because you don't have much experience? Make a loose connection to the question, pull out some background information, and talk about what you need to (see matchups below), like this:

Q) You are not from this field or can U sell insurance ?

> *Numbers have always been fascinating to me. When I was in high school, I watched my mother working our home budget. She taught me how to use Quicken to help manage my allowance. Quicken was like a puzzle to me and I loved solving that puzzle. I'm enrolled in a course in Peachtree this term, carrying an 'A' average. I'm confident I can learn your system quickly.*

Selling have always been fascinating to me. When I was in Godrej, I watched my seniors working on sales target. They taught me how to probe to know what the customer wanted

Highlight All Your Skills

You're the one who wants the job. Be sure you present the complete picture of yourself. It's your right and responsibility to see that all the relevant information about you gets covered during the interview. Much of the information can be inserted as you respond to existing questions. Plan everything you want to be known; then find ways to weave in, push in, or simply add any information that hasn't come up.

For example, the position for which you are interviewing requires these skills and experience: telephone sales, basic bookkeeping, a customer service background, knowledge of the industry, some supervisory experience, and the ability to work without constant supervision. The interviewer seems prepared and she covers all requirements but supervision. The interview is coming to a close. It's your responsibility to get this topic introduced. She asks you to relate something you especially liked about your last job. Frame your response to include your supervisory abilities. Your response could be:

> One of my favorite things about the job at The Neighborhood Home was a chance to work with the high school students who came for their volunteer work. I was asked to give them some basic training in how to listen with sympathy and concern and how to ask questions that kept their senior partner talking. As part of that training I observed their work and wrote short reports on their work. This supervision of young students was challenging for me. And I realized that even though I was young I could supervise others. I was positive in my critiques and the kids were positive to me.

Or, as she closes her folder, she asks, Is there anything you'd like to ask? Realizing that supervision hasn't been mentioned, you can respond:

Your ad mentioned supervision of others. My experience supervising high school volunteers at the senior center was challenging and fun for me. Tell me about the kinds of supervision this job may include.

As she describes the job she is likely to follow up with a question about your experience.

Alternately, she smiles a "We're finishing now!" smile and says, *Would you like to add anything?* Yes, you would:

My experience supervising high school students at the senior center was especially challenging and interesting. This position offers me a chance to continue to grow in skills as a supervisor. Can you tell me a bit about that part of the job?

Note that with all these alternatives you have been careful not to make the interviewer feel she has been inadequate by not covering the supervision qualification.

Matchups Show What Information To Communicate

A successful job interview results from a high percentage of matchups between what the job requires that you possess and what you seek that the position offers. In fact, that's the only kind of job you'd want to accept. If the interviewer is to see those matchups, find them and prepare ways to demonstrate them.

Preparing the matchups also prepares you for the interview. Prepare these matchups with a two-column sheet of paper. In the left column list skills, experience, aptitudes, preferences that the job description indicates are required. Make that list detailed and specific. Add items as you research the company.

List additional aspects which you can assume will be necessary or useful, even though they aren't in the job description, such as people skills, meeting management, computer literacy.

skills, exp
aptitude, preferences
attitude, interests

attitudes & interests
List any background, experiences, skills
training, interests which u hv. to match
-up w/ the left.

Next, list aspects that you deduce will add value to the successful candidate such as attitudes and interests. Attitudes can't be advertised for; yet your love of hiking and camping and a long standing membership in the Sierra Club will make you a more likely candidate for a position in an environmental company. A job selling hearing aids can't require that you wear one yourself, but your traumas and experience from your own hearing aid fitting can an advantage.

Another category is to consider is those topics which are "legally-forbidden-to-ask-but-OK-to-bring-up" such as physical appearance and age. For a front desk position at a talent agency, your attractiveness, great figure, and excellent grooming are qualities that the company may not legally require, but you may bring them up. If the position involves community liaison with elder care programs and senior citizen centers, the company may not legally advertise for or give preference to an older person, but that shouldn't stop you from promoting your maturity.

In the right column, list any background, experiences, skills, training,, interests you have to match up with the items in the left column. For many items the matchup will be obvious and easy. For others, you may have to be more imaginative. What if you want that job as liaison to the senior programs–and you're twenty-three? Figure out why you want the job, and the matchup will usually become apparent. You've grown up around four grandparents, gone on frequent vacations with your grandmother, planted gardens with both granddads, and volunteered at the nursing home near your house for five years; be prepared to say so, up front (and certainly in the application letter–you don't want your application rejected in the first cut because of your youth.) You may also want the job because it seems an easy entry level job for the political career you hope to carve out for yourself. Should you say that too? Perhaps, but not up front. But do write it down; this sheet is your interview preparation.

Here are other examples of imaginative matchup thinking and planning.

The job description indicates the successful candidate will need proven communication skills in a work situation, both written and oral. You do have good communication skills, but they were acquired and practiced primarily during your education – not in a work situation. Your task will be to find a way phrase the educational experience that satisfies the requirement. The interview question is *Tell me about your communication skills* or *How good are your communications skills?* Here are two possible responses:

My communication skills are strong. Our seminar classes in design engineering were all conducted as real businesses. We teamed to research projects, with frequent meetings, we discussed our projects with an instructor, and each of us presented both an oral and a written report on two project during the term. I receive high marks for each phase of the projects, so I feel fully confident to use these skills right away.

or

My communication skills are strong. The best jobs I could get working my way through school were mostly number crunching jobs, because I have had computer and accounting classes. When I needed to clarify instructions or explain a project to my supervisor, I was able to do that easily. My classes in design engineering were all conducted with meetings, oral and written reports, so I have had a chance to "test" my communicating in a business setting. These classes were graded as much on communications as on design, and I got excellent grades.

In each case you have covered the question, given the seeker assurance that you can communicate, and finessed the issue of experience in a work setting. In addition you wove in other strengths: you worked your way through school, you have computer and accounting experience, you have high grades.

Note that in both examples, the opening statement is a strong positive response to the general thrust of the question. Speak with a confident voice to further enhances your strength. As mentioned elsewhere, how you say something is usually at least as important as what you say.

This next example requires more creativity, a bigger adjustment, to make a matchup. The job requires recent work experience in supervision; but your last few years have been spent raising your kids. However, your activity as co-chair of the city-wide Parent Teachers Silent Auction required you to coordinate 6 committees (a total of 47 volunteers) whose duties included donations, fair market prices, and site selection, among others. Though unpaid, that eight-month experience qualifies as "work experience in supervision" – if you have it prepared and phrased that way.

I recruited and organized 47 volunteers into six committees to put on a highly successful Silent Auction for the city-wide Parent Teachers organization. Those eight months of meetings, with their need for organization, guidance, cajoling, encouraging, and pushing were work experience in supervision in the best sense of that term.

In sum, evaluate what you can do, what skills you nov possess, **regardless of how you acquired them.** If you have a skill, you can use it, provided you believe you can, whether you got it in a paid work setting, as a volunteer, in education or as a parent. Just as with all thinking on your feet, answering questions during the interview works best if you are prepared.

Points to Remember

Compare what the position needs with what you offer and prepare those matchups. Get a sheet of paper out now.

14

Gender Speaking Requires Thinking on Your Feet

What do gender communications have to do with thinking on your feet? Everything. First, men and women **tend** to use conversation for vastly different purposes. Successfully communicating with members of the opposite sex requires thinking on your feet every time. Second, communicating with anybody frequently will be easier and more successful if you make a quick assessment and perhaps an adjustment of your usual approach. "Adjustment of your usual approach" are the operative words, because most of us communicate the same way all the time. Yet, some individuals respond best to directness, some to indirectness. Some people want you to get to the point immediately, others want details. Beyond the gender and the personality of the people involved, different circumstances and situations lend themselves to varying amounts of conversation and information.

Matching your style to both the individual and the circumstance, you will create a variety of communicating styles. I call this variety a Conversation Wardrobe ©. The problem is deciding how much to say and how to say it. The solution is to develop a wardrobe of conversational styles and then decide which style of conversation is appropriate in any specific situation. The key is that different situations require different conversational costumes, different approaches and responses. Get back to the basic premise of thinking on your feet, buying time to think. Use those few seconds to select the appropriate costume or style of conversation.

You already have a conversational wardrobe, whether you know it or not. Most of us are probably "wearing" the same thing to every occasion, *i.e.,* employing our usual approach in all conversations. Add new styles to your conversational wardrobe, even update your old style. (Consult my book *How To Talk So Men Will Listen*, published by Contemporary Books, for a complete discussion of the Conversational Wardrobe ©.)

How Male–Female Styles Vary

Men and women have distinct differences in their communicating styles and specifically in their purposes for conversation. Men tend to use conversation to exchange information. Women tend to use conversation to build relationships. Remember when the discussion is of tendencies, the result is generalization. To generalize is to form general notions or conclusions, a common enough practice to deal with large concepts. When I discuss gender differences in speeches, both men and women march up to me with excitement and challenge in their eyes and their voices: *I don't do that!* Of course. People of both genders communicate against type. But your own experiences will support these necessary generalizations.

Men exchange information with their friends about prices, horsepower, batting averages, and cubic yards. They exchange business information about fees, contracts, warranties, flowcharts, and timetables, getting to the bottom line.

When talking with a female friend, a woman is likely to share intimate details about relationships, health of family, mood, goals, and personal difficulties. At work, mindful of the importance of working relationships which facilitate productivity, women will tend to speak of or inquire about staff interactions, promotions, problems people are having with projects.

Men tend to talk about things; women tend to talk about people. In conversations, men contract, women expand. Contracting is saying less than average; expanding is saying more than average. Understanding these basic preferences, recognize the need to adjust your own style to better fit the person to whom you are going to ask a question, make a statement, or respond to a query.

If the question from your male assistant is *What do you want done with the drafts of the Johnson report?* your preference is to think out loud–processing out loud to figure out our decision is a habit women have. Your usual approach might sound like this *Well, I can't remember ever going back to the drafts. But we might want to see how the process of decision making changed. What do you think?* (note another habit of women: ending with a question, rather than a statement, to draw the other into the conversation.) Your assistant want to know what **you** want done. A more successful thinking on your feet response to his question would be *File it for 6 months. If we haven't referred to it in that time, junk it. In fact, please do that with all drafts.*

Women talk more because they want to; men talk less because they want to. Thinking on your feet, you'll select a style that fits your listener, not you.

How Individual Styles Vary

As discussed above, individual styles don't just divide along gender lines. After a recent keynote speech on *How To Talk So Men Will Listen* on the East Coast, a male member of the audience sidled up, with this whispered comment: *Ya know, Marian, when I'm listening I want you to get right to the point, just like you say. But when I'm talking, I go on and on just like women do.* Lots of men love details and relate them with the same length and enthusiasm that women tend to do. And women, particularly women in business, get irate at an individual who takes too long to get to the point as men tend to.

When you communicate on a regular or even an occasional basis with another, it doesn't take long to establish that person's individual style. Once you have established that your female boss gets frustrated at excess explanation, use a concise style with her. Discovering that a male colleague enjoys the minute details of your adventures, give them.

Another aspect of individual style reflects situation: a gifted (read *perceptive*) conversationalist recognizes times to chat and times to get to the bottom line. The best application of the Conversational Wardrobe© is understanding the nuances of individuals, regardless of gender, basing conversational style on the situation or circumstance.

How Circumstances Affect Conversation

When deciding which style from your conversational wardrobe to select for a conversation, the key decisions are basic communicating strategy: provide the explanation first or put the point up front, provide many details or just a few, prioritize or tell all, sit or stand, be assertive or reserved, speak first or wait, work to gain consensus or make your opinion known.

The general tendency is telling too much, because it's our project or problem and we possess both enthusiasm and details. Occasionally we say too little. Once in awhile it's appropriate to tell a long story, spinning the tale out enticingly. More often it's better to relate the just essence of the story. With some narratives save the punch line until the last glorious moment. At other times, resolutely put the point up front. There are circumstances in which to give all the details. At other times (more frequently in business) it's better to prioritize, providing key elements, with only a few details. In certain situations make the point and stop, offering to provide details, but only if they are requested. When we truly want to be heard, there are even times to say nothing.

Level of enthusiasm is important. Showing excitement for a project or a cause helps us capture the imagination of listeners. In such instances, voices typically rise, our delivery of the ideas is speeded up, the words come tumbling out. Such excitement is catching, infectious, positive. Occasionally, however, present a more subdued impression, even a somber one. Maintaining a degree of gravity can keep focus on choosing each word carefully and offering it up with force and with emphasis.

A forward leaning, arms-on-the-table posture generally demonstrates involved, ready to participate. But occasions arise when the situation requires sitting back in our chairs, in a reflective manner, perhaps even reserving judgement or expressing a certain disdain.

When in a conversation with someone whose attention you seek, assertive body language is frequently called for. Looking eye to eye, standing toe to toe, challenges the other and proclaims equality. But there are times when a softer demeanor will pave the way for negotiating.

Using the components of your personal conversational wardrobe, you will be at times gregarious or quiet, filled with details or direct and concise. You'll speak with excitement or comment with restraint. You will speak with confidence, whatever the communicating need, helping move the conversation to its goal.

Points to Remember

Gender doesn't matter so much as appropriate conversational style. Match your communciation skills to the situation.

> ## The TO DO List:
> Assess your existing wardrobe of conversational styles and begin adding other styles today.

15

Other Opportunities to Think on Your Feet

Occasions demand that you think on your feet: discussing a project, being asked to make an impromptu report, making a request or statement. When discussing a project with colleagues, sometimes your mind drifts. Gradually—or suddenly—the conversation shifts to another feature of the project: your feature. Can you take full advantage of this chance to make your point and also make points?

As you attend a meeting, conference, seminar or workshop, you are asked to "say a few words" about a project near to your heart. Sadly, though, it's often less near to your mind. Can you buy enough time to gather your thoughts and make your presence felt?

Introducing Yourself

At conferences and professional lunches you are frequently asked to stand to introduce yourself. What you want and need to say are the basic facts about yourself: name, where you're from, and what your connection to the meeting is. Not exactly difficult or threatening information. A savvy self-introduction may also include a benefit to the audience. Yet most people sound inadequate:

> *uh I'm uh Jack Spratt and uh I own a small print shop. We uh are located on Thirty Fourth Street uh and we'd uh like to have you uh come by.*

or

> *Let's see. My name is Janice Dogood and I'm a consultant and I consult with people about their colors and about their images and I think images are so important and I'm just glad to be here!*

People blow their grand opportunity to make an excellent professional or personal impression in a group that is important to them. The same weak result frequently occurs when people are chatting around a luncheon or banquet table. The same information is exchanged, and people tend to do it poorly. The first question at the table is *What do you do?* As a communications consultant, I'm concerned and aghast at the numbers of professional people who do not have a smooth, professional response to that simple question. Many people give a too short answer: *I'm a lawyer* or *I'm a teacher* or *I sell insurance.* They need to use this opportunity to add one main piece of support, make an impression, begin to build the dialogue that is so important. They can even offer a benefit to the listeners.

Consider:

> *I'm an attorney. My firm specializes in labor relations.*

or

> *I'm in the philosophy department at Mathers Community College. I teach Ethics and Morality.*

or

My firm is XYZ Assurance Company; we can help you with flood coverage for home owners' insurance.

These introductions are better. If you do not like the sound of the word that identifies your profession, rephrase it so you can feel good saying it. I have clients who spent years hating to say that they were "consultants." My solution for them: *I am a partner in a management consulting practice. We specialize in assisting financially troubled companies.* The emphasis is on *partner, management,* and *practice*; the word *consultant* is buried. The second sentence goes on immediately to emphasize a specific area of expertise.

You may hate to say *salesman,* or *teacher,* or "_____." You might begin with the name of your firm and add your role or title second: *I work for Jones and Jones, the environmental engineering firm. I handle the marketing end.*

You can also begin with *My profession is* _____ or *I'm in the* _____ *profession.* Whatever you say, say it with pride and confidence. Avoid the euphemisms that irritate people, such as "sanitation engineer" or "waitperson." Using "waiter," "fisher," "author," "teacher," is appropriate regardless of your gender.

Representing Yourself with Poise

Is this poor representation of ourselves a problem? I think it is. It's a problem because you have specifically put yourself in a situation where you want to make an impression, and then you blow it. We go to conferences and meetings generally because we care about what is going on. The opportunity is ripe for business contacts, marketing, support for ideas, team building. Whether you are a parent seeking support from other parents for your proposal to develop a teen center in your area, a sales rep with a fine product, or a consultant offering your services, the others at the meeting or at your table are all potential allies, clients, or customers. It's a problem easily solved. There are several aspects:

- acknowledge the frustration you feel when you didn't sound like you want to sound.
- resolve to do something to sound more poised.
- script ways to express the three basic items
- practice, practice, practice.

Your introduction should roll smoothly, confidently off your tongue at the drop of a luncheon napkin. Jot down possibilities until you find language that pleases you. Then practice, perhaps while alone in the car.

Saying a Few Words

In situations where you are asked to "say a few words," do just that. Say **a few words.** People babble on at such length that the opportunity becomes a liability. Include the same strategies as for responding to questions. Briefly:

- Buy time by standing up slowly or by walking toward the front of the room.
- Pause to organize your thoughts. Find the one key point that you want to express in this situation.
- Don't open with *Thank you, Martha, for this chance to talk about my favorite project.* Don't waste that key first sentence with emptiness.
- State that one main thought, firmly and with good pauses and emphasis.
- Add one supporting statement or piece of evidence.
- Repeat your point and stop. (And resist saying "thank you" here, too. The audience will remember your last words; those words should be your point.)

As part of your opener, repeat what was requested, for exactly the same reasons you repeat the question when you are part of a group (chapter five):

- buys time to think
- helps you adjust the request to fit your agenda or purpose
- allows you to present a complete piece of information: the request + the statement.

Once in awhile you need to tell bad news. Adopt an indirect approach to soften the blow, perhaps to bury the negative in the middle. Consider this example: Chair of the committee: *Say, Marian, explain for the group why we lost the BCA account.* (I'm foolishly unprepared for this direct hit. I rise slowly from my chair, moving over toward the chair of the Chair, and I say): *Jim, it's very important for us to understand the lessons of the BCA situation. We can improve our next proposal through what we learned.* (You can see that I'm "buying time" here.) *The BCA wanted a precise plan of action, but our team focused on our knowledge of the industry and trends to follow. We'll listen better to the request and also include some early involvement for the next presentation.*

Not bad for thinking on my feet; however, how foolish of me not to have been prepared. Make a habit of considering what you might be asked about prior to a meeting or other function where you may be asked to say a few words about a project. Prepare some words. Assume you will be asked. Have something to say. You'll amaze and impress others with your "impromptu" skills. Powerful people don't wing it, though they appear to; they're prepared to talk about what they're working on.

When a client calls me for some urgent help on damage control he is apt to exclaim, *Was I ever caught off guard by that question!* My reaction tends to be, how can you not be prepared to talk about what you are doing? You run into your supervisor in the coffee lounge. She asks you to give her a quick update on your current task, the Uptown Mall. Adopting another strategy from responding to questions, buy time with a choice question, requiring her to select the aspect she most wants to hear about:

> You: *The Uptown Mall project is progressing nicely. Do you want to hear first about the politics of the project or about the costs?*
>
> Supervisor: *I'm interested primarily in the politics; overseeing the cost side is John's responsibility now.*

If you begin without this choice, you might pick costs, because they are simpler to describe. She would become impatient because you aren't getting to the point—her point. By getting her to make a decision, you improve the possibility that your comments will be what she actually wants to hear about. Including the word *first* is reassuring as it indicates you are ready to talk about either.

Funny One-Liners

What about funny one-liners that you hear people toss off in response to questions? Why haven't those been covered here? Because they're a land mine unless if you are a standup comic. Humor depends for its funniness on poking fun at or ridiculing something or someone. You risk putting down the seeker or someone else in the audience. Having a laugh at the seeker's expense may seem like good fun at the time. And sometimes it appears to work. But it will come back to haunt you.

Some people get away with poking fun at others, because they know the audiences, the seeker, the institution being poked fun at. They are also masters of timing and excellent judges of good taste. The person they make fun of is often themselves. Even then the joke can backfire. Everyone has been disgusted at a speaker for misplaced humor. Trying to be funny when answering questions is too risky unless you're a professional whose goal is to be funny. Your goals are more serious:

- effective communication
- good human relationships
- a poised, confident presentation.

Resolve to practice the tips in this books so you can achieve these goals and become a pro at thinking on your feet.

The TO DO List:

Write out several ways to describe who you are and what you do, with emphasis on different aspects: title, company's purpose, duties. Create one for peers and another for clients or customers. Practice them until you express them smoothly.

Index

About the Author

Marian K. Woodall is the author of four popular books and two audio cassette packages designed to sharpen your communicating, whether one-to-one, with a group, or to a group. She is available to speak or present seminars on the topics of her books and a wide range of other oral communications topics. Her professionalism, enthusiasm, and lively participatory style will involve your audience, highlighting your meeting or conference.